ISBN: 978-0-9855920-9-7

Published by Paolo Terni BriefCoachingSolutions

California, USA

Mr. Bear Wants to Be Loved:

Stories and Activities for Using Solution-Focus in the Classroom.

Dr. Paolo Terni, MAPP, PCC

Table of Contents

Introduction

Solution-Focus (SF) is an evidence-based approach for facilitating change.
It is used in therapy, coaching and consulting (see the last chapter).
The purpose of this book is to help teachers use SF strategies in the classroom.

STRUCTURE

In this book you will find nine *stories*:
- Stories one through three illustrate some SF assumptions about change and learning;
- Stories four through six illustrate how to use SF to facilitate self-directed learning in the classroom;
- Stories seven through nine illustrate some SF strategies that can be used to facilitate behavioral change in the classroom.

One or more classroom *activity* accompanies each story, for a total of 18 activities.
Evidence supports the effectiveness of each activity, either directly or indirectly.
Directly: researchers tested the activity in an elementary or middle school setting and achieved positive outcomes.
Indirectly: researchers successfully tested a similar intervention with older populations, such as high school students or working adults. I adapted the activity for use with younger students, making the

educated guess that it would work with them as well. However reasonable it is to assume that an activity that works, for example, with high school students might work with middle schools students (after making the necessary tweaks), that is still an untested assumption. Further research is needed.

In addition to stories and activities, each chapter includes:

- *Comments* that make explicit the point of the story and that elaborate on Solution-Focus (SF) ideas;
- *Questions* that incorporate the moral of the story. Teachers can use the questions to engage students or for their own self-reflection;
- One *Quote* that summarizes the key concept presented in the story;
- *References* for the activities and ideas presented in the chapter.

CHARACTERS

In this book we follow Ms. Elephant and Mr. Monkey while they are helping characters who want to make a change in their lives.

Mr. Monkey is very well intentioned, and he tries to help the forest's inhabitants following the traditional, or problem-focused, approach to change.

Ms. Elephant is very well intentioned too. She helps the forest's inhabitants by empowering them using a SF approach.

On Catching the Big Wave

Assumption One: Useful Change Is Always Happening.

Ms. Elephant and Mr. Monkey are sitting on the beach, enjoying the sunset.

Mr. Monkey says, "Look, Ms. Elephant! A swimmer!"

There it was, in the choppy waters -- a swimmer.

With each powerful stroke after powerful stroke, the swimmer was slowly getting closer to the beach.

Fighting the waves, the swimmer was making a lot of effort.

Mr. Monkey says, "Fighting hard and with a lot of effort. This is how you make progress in life."

Ms. Elephant says, "Look, Mr. Monkey! A surfer!" And there it was, riding the choppy waves -- a surfer.

Swiftly and elegantly, the surfer was zooming towards the beach.

Riding a big wave, the surfer seemed to be making hardly any effort.

Ms. Elephant says, "Riding the waves of change that are already moving in the right direction. This, too, is how you make progress in life."

COMMENTS:

Swimming represents the most common way of thinking about making progress: you use muscle-power to propel yourself forward. That is indeed valuable. Students need to apply willpower, discipline and persistence to learn. It takes effort.

Surfing represents another way of thinking about making progress: you use what is there to power yourself forward.

Learning new things is hard, true. But sometimes teachers can make learning easier by leveraging any small signs they can see in students that point in the right direction.

For example, a child who loves dinosaurs might be more likely to learn biology if the teacher makes the effort to help the student see the connection between biology and dinosaurs. So, what is each student in your class mostly interested in? Is there anything that feeds their curiosity or anything that turns them on academically?

The same reasoning applies to behavioral change. However disruptive some children are, if you pay attention you will notice that there are times when these very same children are quiet and miraculously behaving, even if only for a few minutes. How can you, as a teacher, "ride" on this wave? What is different in those situations? What do you, and the child, need to do differently so that there are more of these "good" times?

Lastly, the same applies to academic performance. Even if most of the time a few students perform badly, there might be times when these very same students do a little bit better. What was different then? How can you help them to do more of whatever worked for them in those situations?

In this book I will provide structured activities to systematically ask the questions listed above, and much more, in an effort to give you the tools to approach your students in a different way, a Solution-Focused way (SF; see the last chapter: "What is Solution-Focus?").

The basic assumption of SF is that useful change is always happening. True, often it is necessary to set boundaries, enforce discipline and use assertive ways to make change happen; and sometimes the best course of action might simply be to notice small changes in the right direction and build on them.

Activity One: What is Working (WW).

The goal of this activity is to develop your abilities to see what is working in each student of your class.

It is an exercise for your own development, and it does not involve any specific interaction with the class or with individual students.

There are many different ways to structure this activity. Below are some suggested options. Feel free to build your own.

1) **Checklist**. Make a list of all your students with a checkbox next to each name. When you see a student doing something right (for example, raising her hand when she wants to speak), check the box next to that student's name. Your goal is to make sure that by the end of the day you have checked the box next to <u>each</u> student's name. When it gets easier, you can challenge yourself and put two, three or more boxes next to each student's name. HOWEVER, first make sure that you have at least one box checked next to EACH student's name before moving on to adding two boxes. It might be easier to check boxes next to some students' names than others, so stick with this process. Do not keep adding checks next to, say, Asdrubale's name while Gioconda's is still empty. If you got a positive observation for each student except for Gioconda, focus on her until her box is checked. Then, and only then, you can add another layer of boxes to check.

2) **Focus group**. Each day, select three students and no more than three. Then, during the day and unbeknownst to them, notice all that they do right. If you manage to write these observations down, during class or right after, even better. Each day change the students you are focusing on until you go through the whole class.

3) **Surprise**! Each week, select three students and no more than three. Then, during the week and unbeknownst to them, pay attention to each time they surprise you positively, for example by turning in a

good homework or by behaving in class for a whole day. Write your observations and your reflections at the end of each week.

Regardless of what format you use, at the end of the activity ask yourself what you would be doing differently as a consequence of your observations.

Furthermore, even though you are not going to directly involve the class in this activity, the observations you collect can be extremely useful for carrying out other activities you find in this book (for example activity eight, "Compliments", included in the chapter "Mr. Bear Wants To Be Loved").

USEFUL QUESTIONS FOR TEACHERS:

- What is better today about student X? What else is better?
- Have there been times recently when things were going the way you wanted with student X, even a little bit or for a little while? What was happening? What did you do differently? How did student X respond differently? How did you react to his or her response, then?
- What would be the first small signs that would tell you that student X is doing a little bit better? What would you be doing then that you are not doing now? What would other students notice? How would they respond?

QUOTE:

The whole universe is change and life itself is but what you deem it.

-- Marcus Aurelius

KEY CONCEPT:

Useful Change Is Always Happening.

FURTHER READING:

Berg, I. K., & Szabo, P. (2005). *Brief coaching for lasting solutions.* New York: Norton.

Mr. Bird Builds a Nest

Assumption Two: The Problem Solver Is the Expert.

Mr. Bird wants to build a wonderful place for his beloved Mrs. Bird. So he goes to Mr. Monkey and asks him, "Mr. Monkey, I want to build a special place for Mrs. Bird. How can I do that?"

Mr. Monkey tells Mr. Bird, "Easy! You need to build her a big house."

Mr. Bird replies, "I only know how to build nests. How do you build a house?"

Mr. Monkey says, "Easy! Dig a deep hole. Then put in a strong foundation. Then build walls with wood. Then make windows. Then make a roof!"

But Mr. Bird is small!

His beak cannot dig a deep hole.

His tiny claws cannot put together walls.

He has never built a house before! He only knows how to build nests!

An unhappy Mr. Bird flies away.

17

Mr. Bird then goes to Ms. Elephant and says, "Ms. Elephant, I want to build a special place for Mrs. Bird. How can I do that?"

Ms. Elephant asks Mr. Bird, "What would a special place for Mrs. Bird look like?"

Mr. Bird replies, "Oh, it would be all shiny and sparkly! But I do not know how to build a house!"

Ms. Elephant asks, "Mr. Bird, what do you know how to build?"

A proud Mr. Bird replies, "I build beautiful nests!

My beak picks up little twigs.

My tiny claws allow me to hold onto a tree and to weave the little twigs together.

I know how to build nests!"

Ms. Elephant asks, "Mr. Bird, how would you make a shiny and sparkly nest?"

Mr. Bird replies, "I would put some sparkly objects here and there as I weave the nest together.

A piece of shiny glass here.

A chewing-gum wrapper there.

It will be beautiful!"

Having found his answer, an excited and happy Mr. Bird flies away.

COMMENTS:

In Solution-Focus (SF) practice, we say "the client is the expert".

That means that clients decide what is best for them; and that a SF practitioner does not provide solutions but instead helps clients build their own unique solutions.

This approach has two important benefits: the first is that the client is more invested in making the solution happen, because it is his or her solution; the second is that the solution is based on what the client already knows how to do, not on what the practitioner think is the right solution because it is what he or she knows how to do. Too often we forget that our skills and expertise and knowledge are not universal; and that is why making hard things simple is a difficult skill. We call it teaching.

The belief that "the student is the expert" is at the core of many teaching approaches, such as the following:

- Meeting students where they are. That means using language that is easily understandable to that specific class. That also means adopting a lesson format that best supports the learning of those specific students. The specific class you are teaching determines what constitutes the right kind of language and the right kind of approach, and that is why in the prompts for the activities in this book I often include the qualifier "use most appropriate language" or "age appropriate language".

- Understanding and echoing back, if appropriate, students' lingo. One of the best ways to adapt to students is to notice how they speak. For example, notice key words or phrases, and use them when appropriate. At the very least, be curious about them.

- Believing that, as experts on their own lives, each student has developed unique strengths and skills, often in challenging environments. In this book many activities are centered on observing, eliciting and building on students' resources. You can find one such activity below. Even if it might be difficult to spot strengths in some students, make an effort -- there is plenty there to see. For example, if someone just shows up for class but does not participate actively, start with the fact that she actually shows up. It might be an achievement in itself in some disadvantaged settings. How does she manage to do that? Or maybe one of your students is very good at causing mayhem in class. How does he do that? How can you and the class use or redirect that energy?

- Making sure that you understand why something is a problem or a desired goal for the student; and conversely, making sure that the student understands why something is a problem or could be a desired goal. For example, sometimes we might not understand why something, say a reproach, is such a big deal for a student. If we believe that students are the experts on their own lives, then obviously the student has good reasons to be upset. So what are those reasons?

If you are perplexed about students' behaviors, ask them what makes them think that the chosen course of action is a good idea. Help them consider the point of view of all the stakeholders involved, including other students.

Activity Two: Three Words.

You can carry out this activity in at least two different ways:

1) As a solo activity. Think about each student and write down how you would describe him or her using three positive attributes. You can use personality traits (e.g., conscientious or extroverted), character strengths (e.g., kind or zestful), identities (e.g., an athlete or a scholar), or anything else (e.g. always smiling). It does not matter. What matters is that the three characteristics are positive.

2) As an individual activity for students. Ask students to write down three positive words that define them. If helpful, ask them how their loved ones would describe them in three words. Once they have these words, invite students to write a short essay regarding one time when they exhibited that quality. What happened? What did they do? Why does that show kindness, or creativity, or perseverance?

Activity Three: School Crafting.

Researchers found that in most jobs workers have some degree of control over their activities. For example, employees can re-arrange their tasks, change the tasks' scope or change how activities are done. So why not do that strategically to reflect their own passions, values and interests? In other words, workers can craft their own job while remaining within the given organizational parameters. Job crafting leads to increased engagement, increased work satisfaction and ultimately enhanced well-being.

How about "school crafting"?

True, there are currently no tested "student crafting" exercises directly derived from job crafting that I am aware of.

However, we can try to adapt the core intuition of job crafting to the classroom. What follows are some suggestions for experimentation.

Experimentation one:

1) Have students identify one school subject they like best and why (for example: history, because I like stories).

2) Next, first in small groups and then in class as a whole, discuss how they can inject more of that subject into their school day or their homework, to make it more interesting. For example, when the class is learning about subtraction of negative numbers, the

student who likes history might look up who first came up with that idea and then tell the story to the class.

Teachers here have a key role to play in suggesting how students could be doing more of what they like even in subjects that are not the most appealing to students.

Experimentation two:

1) Have students reflect on how they learn best. For example, by listening to instructions or by reading aloud or by working with a peer.

2) Then, first in small groups and then in class as a whole, discuss how they can do more of that strategy when learning. For example, when learning about subtraction of negative numbers, the student who likes to listen can record the instructions on how to do that, and play them again and again as he solves negative numbers problems at home. Or if she likes reading aloud, she might read aloud the problem and each step she is taking to solve it when she is doing her math homework.

Activity Four: What If.

This is an open ended prompt for you.

Whenever you are creating a lesson plan, ask yourself: what if my students were the experts on learning this?

How would I involve them? How would they leverage their strengths and expertise as learners?

The goal is to create opportunities for you to be creative in leveraging students' strengths, skills and interests.

USEFUL QUESTIONS FOR TEACHERS:

- [To student]: Suppose somehow this difficulty disappears; what would you be doing differently? [sometimes students and adults alike get stuck on something, without realizing that there is a lot they can do without tackling the problem directly].
- [To student]: What would a solution to this problem look like? How could your best friend X tell that you solved this problem?
- [To student]: What has worked for you in similar situations in the past? What else?
- [To student]: What are you good at? What would your friends say you are good at? How can you use that in the current situation?
- [To student]: I noticed you are good at X. How can you use that ability in this situation?

QUOTE:

Despite life's struggles, all persons possess strengths that can be marshaled to improve the quality of their lives.
-- Insoo Kim Berg

KEY CONCEPT:

People Are the Experts on Their Own Lives.

FURTHER READING:

Regarding the presupposition that "the client is the expert": De Jong, P., & Berg, I. K. (2012). *Interviewing for solutions* (3rd ed.). Belmont, CA: Cengage Learning.

Regarding the Three Words exercise: Roberts, L. M., Dutton, J. E., Spreitzer, G. M., Heaphy, E. D., & Quinn, R. E. (2005). Composing the reflected best-self portrait: Building pathways for becoming extraordinary in work organizations. *Academy of Management Review, 30*(4), 712-736.

Regarding job crafting, a good introductory article can be found here: https://hbr.org/2010/06/managing-yourself-turn-the-job-you-have-into-the-job-you-want. For a more formal take, the original paper is the following: Wrzesniewski, A., & Dutton, J. E. (2001). Crafting a job: Revisioning employees as active crafters of their work. *Academy of Management Review, 26*(2), 179-201.

On Challenges: the Waterfall
Assumption Three: It Takes Practice

Adriano and Alessandro are two salmon.

Adriano makes it over the waterfall.

Adriano thinks he did it because he is very smart.

Adriano would like to go over the next waterfall, to see what is there.

But the waterfall is high.

Adriano is afraid that he might not make it on his first try.

Adriano is afraid if he does not make it on his first try, it means he is stupid.

So Adriano chooses not to try.

He remains in his little lake, always wondering what is there beyond it.

Alessandro makes it over the waterfall.

Alessandro thinks he did it because he worked very hard.

Alessandro would like to go over the next waterfall, to see what is there.

But the waterfall is high.

Alessandro is not afraid that he might not make it on his first try.

Alessandro knows that if he does not make it on his first try, it does not mean he is stupid.

It just means he needs to work more on it and do something different.

So Alessandro chooses to try.

He does not make it on his first try; there was a big rock on the left!

But now that he knows this, he tries again by jumping to the right!

He makes it! He is now in a different, bigger and nicer lake, farther upstream.

New challenges and discoveries await him.

COMMENTS:

One of the main factors that sets apart excellent performers from average performers is the amount of practice. True, some students seem to be more talented -- they are the Ferraris in the classroom. Some other students might seem slower -- they are the station wagons in the classroom. However, even a station wagon can get to destination sooner if its driver keeps on going while the driver of the Ferrari stops to play video games.

There is more: station wagons can grow into Ferraris, if they have a growth mindset. The growth mindset is the belief that our abilities are not fixed, but can grow over time -- if we put in enough effort and practice. If you have a growth mindset, then, effort is not a sign that you are not cut out for it; rather, it is a sign that you are growing. Similarly, if you have a growth mindset, you see mistakes as part of the process of learning, not as a sign that you reached the ceiling of your capabilities.

It is a good idea then to praise students for their efforts instead of for their traits. If they do not manage to accomplish a task, invite them to try again, maybe in a different way, until they get it done. If they do manage to accomplish a task, again praise them on their efforts and do not attribute their success to fixed traits such as intelligence. If you do, then they may be less likely to try more difficult tasks. After all, now they have something to lose: your assessment that they are intelligent.

Activity Five: Fostering a Growth Mindset.

1) Talk to your class about the fact that the brain, just like a muscle, grows with learning. We are not born smart; we become smart by embracing challenges. If feasible, integrate your talk with a Youtube video about the growth mindset: if you search for "Growth Mindset for Students" you can find several helpful videos; pick the one that is most age appropriate. You can also find a lesson plan developed by Stanford University researchers here: https://www.khanacademy.org/coach-res/reference-for-coaches/how-to/a/growth-mindset-lesson-plan.

2) After your general introduction, with or without video, share your own experience with the growth mindset. Share a story about a challenge you faced and that eventually you met successfully. Be sure to highlight the following: that you had to work hard (after all, even surfers might try different small waves and fail before finally finding and riding the big one; and it took them time and effort to become surfers in the first place!); that you had to find the right strategy to overcome the challenge (maybe by looking at what worked in the past for you); and that other people helped you, either directly or indirectly. Connect your story with the video shown or the ideas presented when introducing the growth mindset.

3) Invite students to share similar stories in small groups. What challenge did they overcome by not giving up and persisting? How did they find the right

strategy to succeed? Who helped and how? It could be any topic ranging from multiplication of negative numbers to learning a basketball shot to baking cookies.

4) Have a class discussion about what was particularly helpful in overcoming challenges. Make sure to draw a distinction between persisting and blindly following the same strategy again and again (see the chapter: "Mr. Buffalo and the Tree Stump").

5) Ask students to write a letter to a future student (set a minimum number of sentences) in which they describe their own struggle and eventual success. Make sure that the letter includes specific advice on how to overcome challenges when learning something new.

USEFUL STATEMENTS FOR TEACHERS:

- I am so impressed by how hard you worked at this!

- You succeeded, congratulations! I know you put a lot of hard work into this, and it paid off; I was particularly impressed by how you went from having challenges with moving decimal places to mastering it!

- Even though we are not there yet, I am impressed by how hard you worked at it. How can you tweak your efforts to achieve better results next time?

QUOTE:
There is no failure, only feedback.
-- Robert Allen

KEY CONCEPT:
The Growth Mindset.

FURTHER READING:
Dweck, C. (2006). *Mindset: The new psychology of success.* New York: Random House.

You can also find a good introduction to the Growth Mindset at the Character Lab webpage: https://characterlab.org/resources/growth-mindset.

Mr. Bear Wants to Be Loved

Ingredient of Change: Confidence.

Mr. Bear is sitting by the path.

He is resting his head on his paws, all sad.

Mr. Monkey greets him, "Hello, Mr. Bear! Why are you sad?"

Mr. Bear replies, "Because all the animals are afraid of me."

Mr. Monkey asks, "Why are they afraid of you? What did you do?"

An upset Mr. Bear replies, "I did not do anything wrong, Mr. Monkey! I am good and I love the other animals of the forest! They are afraid of me because ... I am a bear!"

"Indeed you are!" Mr. Monkey declares.

And with those words, Mr. Monkey just leaves.

Ms. Elephant then comes along.

Mr. Bear is still sitting by the path.

He is still resting his head on his paws, and he looks even sadder now.

Ms. Elephant greets him, "Hello, Mr. Bear! What's going on?"

Mr. Bear replies, "I am so sad because I am a bear and all animals are afraid of me."

Ms. Elephant kindly asks, "Am I afraid of you, Mr. Bear?"

Mr. Bear replies, "No, Ms. Elephant -- but you are so big!"

Ms. Elephant asks, "Mr. Monkey is smaller than you. Was he afraid to talk to you?"

"No he was not!" a more animated Mr. Bear replies.

Ms. Elephant kindly asks, "Mr. Bird is even smaller. Was he afraid asking for your help when he had it in his mind he needed to build a house?"

"No he was not!" Mr. Bear replies.

Ms. Elephant asks again, "Mrs. Raccoon is afraid of you. But does she know that you leave the small berries for her, when you go pick berries?"

Mr. Bear replies, "No she does not. But I can let her know!"

An energized and smiling Mr. Bear gets up and starts dancing!

So from that moment on, Mr. Bear never stayed again by the side of the path, sad.

Realizing that many animals did not fear him, Mr. Bear got the confidence he needed to let them know he loved them.

To this day, if anyone in the forest needs help, they go to Mr. Bear.

Mr. Bear is now very happy.

And he goes picking berries with Mrs. Raccoon.

COMMENTS:

Confidence in the fact that change can happen can be greatly increased by simply noticing instances of useful change already happening.

When students realize that they are already changing in the desired direction, maybe even just a little bit, they become much more confident about seeing the change through.

Activity Six: Resource Exercise.

Every week (preferred option) or at the end of each school day, have students write down and share up to three things that they are grateful for; or that they are proud they achieved over the week.

You can do this activity focusing on the following:

- Individual learning, for example:

What are you grateful / happy / proud that you learned this week / today?

Why?

How did you manage to do that?

- Social appreciation, for example:

What are three things your classmates did over the week/ day that you are grateful for / proud of?

What were the positive effects of your classmates' actions?

- Achievement, for example:

What are you grateful / happy / proud you achieved this day/week?

Why?

How did you manage to do that?

Or you can do this activity by maintaining a broader focus, for example:

What are you grateful for this week/today?

Activity Seven: Progress Milestones.

Make sure that your students keep a record of their milestones. Every month (or whenever it makes sense), have a "progress milestone party" when you invite them to think about the progress made:

- Have them review the month;

- Have them identify the milestones reached, the goals achieved;

- Have them share them in class or in small groups;

- You can encourage them with questions such as: "Remember when you could not do X? Now look at you!"

- Have them write a paragraph of encouragement and advice to their past selves. Thinking of themselves a month ago, what advice would they give to themselves? How did they manage to achieve their milestones? How did they persevere? What was the secret of their success?

Activity Eight: Compliments.

Confidence about making progress can also be increased quickly by giving compliments every now and then. Whenever appropriate, directly or indirectly draw attention to:

- What a specific student is doing right; for example, "Look at you going through these math problems, I am really impressed by your focus!"

- What a specific student did right in the past; for example, "I was really impressed by how last week you managed to write that beautiful essay even though it was a topic you struggled with at first, well done!"

- What a specific student is doing partially right; for example, a student raises her hand and offers an answer to a question, but it is the wrong answer: "Mary, that was a good try, and we can learn only by trying different things; we are on the right track, how about carrying over that number all the way, instead of only one decimal place, what do you say?"

Tips:

a) Solution-Focused practitioners often use the following 3-point format when giving compliments:

- "*I am impressed by* [insert here the specific desired behavior that you observed, e.g., getting an answer right],

- "*Because* [specific reason why you are impressed, e.g., you know the student struggles with that topic]

- "*And that allowed you / the class / us to*" [positive effects of the behavior observed].

It is not always necessary to follow all these steps and you are welcome to come up with different variations on the wording. It is, however, a good starting point for structuring your compliments.

b) Positive Psychology practitioners often use <u>Active Constructive Responding (ACR)</u>.

Responses to good behaviors, e.g., a right answer, can fall in any of the following categories:

- Passive Constructive: "Good".

- Passive Destructive: "Who else?"

- Active Destructive: "Perfect example of how a broken clock can be right twice a day".

- Active Constructive: "Great job, I'm so happy you remembered this concept, I know you worked hard on this, keep it up!"

Obviously the goal is to respond in an Active Constructive way, keeping in mind that what qualifies the response as Active Constructive is not only what you say but how you say it.

USEFUL QUESTIONS and STATEMENTS FOR TEACHERS:

- [To student]: Thinking of what you achieved so far, what tells you that this problem can be solved?
- [To student]: Have there been times recently when there were little signs of progress in learning this?

- [To student]: How did you manage to do that? Where did you learn that?
- [To student]: I am really impressed by how...

QUOTE:

What we pay attention to, and how we pay attention, determines the content and quality of life.

-- Csíkszentmihályi Mihály

KEY CONCEPT:

Notice What is Working and Give Compliments to Increase Confidence.

FURTHER READING:

Regarding the Resource and Compliments activities: Szabó, P. & Meier, D. (2009). *Coaching plain and simple.* New York: Norton.

Regarding the Progress Milestones activity: Amabile, T., & Kramer, S. (2011). *The progress principle: Using small wins to ignite joy, engagement, and creativity at work.* Harvard Business Press.

Regarding Active Constructive Responding: Gable, S. L., Reis, H. T., Impett, E. A., & Asher, E. R. (2004). What do you do when things go right? The intrapersonal and interpersonal benefits of sharing positive events. *Journal of Personality and Social Psychology, 87*(2), 228.

Mr. Boar and His Preferred Future

Ingredient of Change: Attractiveness of Vision.

Mr. Monkey runs into Mr. Boar.

"Hello Mr. Boar!", says a cheerful Mr. Monkey.

"Hello Mr. Monkey," replies Mr. Boar.

Mr. Monkey asks, "Mr. Boar, you look sad. What is wrong?"

Mr. Boar replies, "Oh, well, I am tired of spending my days with my nose in the ground, eating these boring old roots. All I want is some raspberry, they told me I would find them someday, but nothing so far. I am really tired of this."

Mr. Monkey asks, "And why are you tired of that?"

Mr. Boar replies, "It is so dark in the thick forest, where I look for food. Sigh."

Mr. Monkey asks, "Why is it dark in the forest?"

Mr. Boar says, "Because there are many trees and bushes and leaves."

Mr. Boar resumes looking for food, feeling sad.

Mr. Monkey goes away, thinking that Mr. Boar is very strange indeed.

Then Ms. Elephant comes along.

"Hello Mr. Boar!" says a happy Ms. Elephant.

"Hello Ms. Elephant," says Mr. Boar.

A concerned Ms. Elephant inquires, "Mr. Boar, you look sad. What is going on, my friend?"

Mr. Boar sighs and says, "Oh, well, I am tired of spending my days with my nose in the ground, looking for food, in the thick and dark forest, hoping someday to find a raspberry patch that might not even exist."

Ms. Elephant quickly grabs Mr. Boar with her trunk and gently puts him on a strong branch, high on a tree.

Mr. Boar is very surprised!

From the tree Mr. Boar could see far away.

The clouds, so beautiful up in the blue sky!

The sunshine, so warm and bright.

There, in the distance -- right there on the hilltop -- Mr. Boar could see the most amazing and biggest raspberry fields he had ever seen in his life! He is so happy.

Swiftly and adroitly, Ms. Elephant grabs Mr. Boar again and gently puts him back on the ground.

An excited Mr. Boar declares, "Thank you, Ms. Elephant! I know what I have to do to be happy!"

Mr. Boar kept following the paths in the dark forest with renewed energy, until he made it to the hilltop, where he lived happily ever after -- enjoying the clear blue sky, the view and the yummy raspberries.

COMMENTS:

Students might feel at times like Mr. Boar, trudging in a dark forest of repetitive and boring tasks, day in and day out, without a clear idea of how what they are doing might be useful in the future. Math, anyone?

One way to help students persist in their unpleasant but important tasks is to create with them a destination postcard, that is a vivid and attractive picture of what is possible in the future if they keep learning.

Activity Nine: Postcards from the Future.

At the beginning of the school year, pretend for one morning that it is actually the start of the next school year. They are now one grade ahead (so if you are teaching fifth grade, they are now sixth graders; and if the school year starts in 2016, pretend it is 2017).

Tell them all the things they will have learned by then, by sharing with them the learning goals for the year as if these goals had been achieved. Congratulate them warmly.

First in small groups and then with the whole class, invite contributions around the following questions and ideas, providing context when necessary:

- Now that they are sixth graders (if they are actually in fifth grade now), what is it that they are doing differently regarding schoolwork or homework? What makes them accomplished learners?

- Considering what they achieved during the past school year, what are they most proud of?

- What would their families be most proud of?

- How would they know that the school year went well? What else?

- What is it that they enjoyed the most to learn?

- What is it that they are most proud they learned, even though it was difficult? How did they do that?

- What sustained their perseverance and their interest?

- Who helped them along the way? How did they manage to have help and support?

Collect the answers in writing on post-its, or feel free to involve students in activities such as creating an artwork that contains the main points of the discussion.

The goal is to have a poster or similar in the classroom that is officially referred to as the "destination postcard" or "postcard from the future". You can then go back to it, when appropriate, to re-focus students' efforts.

Note: you can extend the timeframe as appropriate. For example, you can tell them that they have now graduated from elementary school or from college! The important idea is to engage students in terms of a journey from where they are to where they want to be. Similarly, praise is best formulated in relation to the destination than in terms of how pleasing their behaviors are to you. For example, the following praise, "I am impressed by how much progress you are making towards becoming a scholar! Offering reasons for your opinion is exactly what scholars do!" is better than stating, "I am so pleased that you provided reasons for your opinion, that is exactly what I asked you to do".

Activity Ten: Working On What Works (WOWW), part one.

The first step of this activity is to agree with the students on something you all want. For example, you might agree that you want to learn in a "good" classroom.

The second step is to figure out what makes a classroom good.

So ask the students, and add your input as appropriate.

For example, you might all agree that what makes a classroom good is that everybody is kind to and respectful of each other and that everybody is paying attention to the teacher.

Collect all the inputs on the blackboard or similar.

In the case of criteria that are not well specified in terms of behavior, such as the ones listed above as examples, it is useful to go for more details.

So if "being respectful of each other" is one of the criteria chosen, then ask your students how they would know they are treating each other with respect. You might then have a list of specific behaviors such as "we do not interrupt each other when talking"; or "we use please and thank you when asking for something". If "paying attention" is one of the criteria chosen, you might then have a list with items such as "we track the teacher with our eyes".

At this point, you have a good picture of the destination, your raspberry hill. That in itself is something very useful, a desired learning environment that the class can be reminded of when appropriate.

In the next chapter, you will find part two of this activity.

Activity Eleven: Boring But Important.

Research shows that helping students connect what they are doing with their own interests and goals can enhance motivation and persistence on difficult or boring tasks.

For example, if a student wants to become a video game designer, the teacher can emphasize how learning basic math builds the logical skills necessary for computer programming. If a student is interested in dinosaurs, the teacher can emphasize how learning about biology is an important part of understanding how dinosaurs lived.

Connecting students' interests with specific classroom activities is a good strategy, but obviously can be done only individually; not all students are interested in the same topics.

To involve the whole class, you can use the following intervention aimed at developing students' self-transcendent purpose for learning.

First, ask the class how the world could be a better place.

You can use the following prompt: "How could the world be a better place? Sometimes the world isn't fair, and so everyone thinks it could be better in one way or another. Some people want there to be less hunger, some want less prejudice, and others want less violence or disease. Other people want lots of other changes. What are some ways that you think the world could be a better place?"

Let students work in small groups.

Then discuss their group work with the whole class. Invite contributions; compliment students for their observations, and amplify their points if appropriate.

Once several good ideas are on the table and the students are engaged, switch to an individual task.

Ask each student to write one or two sentences about how they, individually, think the world could be a better place, given all that the class talked about.

Once done with the individual task, tell the class that students "just like them" are motivated to do well in school not only to have a future career they can enjoy, but also so they can make a positive contribution to the world. You can then share with them any examples you might have of past students who expressed a desire to do something that matters in the future as a motivation for doing well in school today.

For the final step, ask your students to write a paragraph for a future student. They must include at least two sentences that capture their reasons for learning; more specifically, they need to address how learning in school can help them be the kind of person they want to be or how learning can help them make the kind of impact they want to have on the people around them and on society in general.

A similar intervention with high school and college students showed significant effects on their persistence with boring math tasks and with reviewing questions for a test.

USEFUL QUESTIONS:

- [To the student who says what he or she does not want to happen]: What would you like to happen instead?
- [To student]: Suppose you manage to stop doing X [unwanted behavior]. What would you be doing instead?
- [To student]: Suppose you somehow manage to achieve your goal. How would that make a difference? What would you be doing differently? What would your classmates notice you doing differently?
- [To student]: Let's do an experiment. Today act <u>as if</u> you are the student you want to be (e.g., as if you had more self-confidence). What are you doing differently? How do your classmates respond? What are they doing differently?

QUOTE:

He who has a why to live for can bear almost any how.
-- Nietsche

KEY CONCEPT:

Instead of Digging into the Problem, Create Attractive and Detailed Pictures of the Future.

FURTHER READING:

Regarding the idea of Postcards from the Future: Heath, C. & Heath. D. (2010). *Switch: How to change things when change is hard.* New York: Random House. For a more comprehensive but more technical read on the topic: De Shazer, S., Dolan, Y., Korman, H., Trepper, T., McCollum, E., & Berg, I.K. (2007). *More than miracles: The state of the art of solution-focused brief therapy.* Binghamton, NY: The Haworth Press.

Regarding the activity Working On What Works (WOWW): Berg, I.K., & Shilts, L. (2004). *Classroom solutions: WOWW approach.* Milwaukee, MI: BFTC Press.

Regarding the activity Boring But Important: Yeager, D. S., Henderson, M., Paunesku, D., Walton, G., Spitzer, B., D'Mello, S., & Duckworth, A.L. (2014). Boring but important: A self-transcendent purpose for learning fosters academic self-regulation. *Journal of Personality and Social Psychology, 107*(4), 559-580.

Ms. Squirrel and the Stream

Ingredient of Change: Clarity About the Next Step.

Ms. Squirrel is trying to get across a stream.

But it is so big!

And she is so small!

Despite all, she really wants to get across the stream.

Mr. Monkey sees her and wants to help.

He says, "We need to think hard about why you can't make it across.

Maybe you need a boat ...

Maybe you need to be bigger ...

Maybe you need to learn to swim ...

Maybe you need to really want it ..."

But all that thinking hard does not help!

Ms. Squirrel is still stuck, and now she also has an headache!

Ms. Elephant comes along.

It would be easy for Ms. Elephant to carry Ms. Squirrel across the stream.

But Ms. Elephant knows that, despite being small, Ms. Squirrel is very resourceful.

Ms. Elephant goes to her and in doing so she gets her feet wet.

"Dear Ms. Squirrel!" says Ms. Elephant, "I noticed you are already in the stream! I had to step into the water to come here to where you are. The rock you are standing on is already part of the way across!"

Ms. Squirrel says, "You are right, Ms. Elephant! I jumped there and there, on those rocks, so I got here! Three jumps!"

Ms. Elephant smiles and says, "I am very impressed by your jumping skills, Ms. Squirrel."

"Thank you!" Ms. Squirrel says, smiling back.

Ms. Elephant asks, "What if you keep on doing small jumps?"

Ms. Squirrel says, "Ms. Elephant, you are right. I could jump on this rock." Ms. Squirrel jumps on the rock.

"Then on this log." She jumps on the log.

"Then on this other rock." She jumps on the other rock.

"Now I can make a leap to the other side of the stream!"

Ms. Squirrel makes it to the other side of the stream!

Ms. Squirrel thanks Ms. Elephant and goes on her business.

Ms. Elephant is very happy to see how Ms. Squirrel managed to do it all by herself, and she resumes her stroll in the forest.

COMMENTS:

Sometimes we are stuck because the gap between where we are and where we want to be seems huge.

Gaps get covered in a very simple way: one step at a time.

So the way forward is simply to be clear about the next step and to take it; and then do the same for the next one; and so on, until we reach the goal.

Using this approach, we don't need to ever worry about the huge gap, but only about the very small, and doable, next step.

Change becomes manageable this way.

Activity Twelve: Working On What Works (WOWW), part two.

The second part of WOWW is all about using a scale that goes from 1 to 10 to measure progress (see the section below: useful questions).

For example, if the agreed upon goal is that of "being respectful of each other" (see part one of this exercise in the previous chapter), ask the whole class where they think they are regarding this topic on a scale of 1 to 10. Ten would be the most respectful class of students ever, and 1 would be the opposite of that.

There will be some confusion and back and forth, but at some point the class will start converging on a number, let's say 7.

Write that number on the blackboard or similar and then ask students to recall recent examples of respectful behaviors: after all they said they are on a 7, not on a 1, so there must be something good going on.

Collect as many examples as you can. Keep eliciting stories from students by doing the following: keep asking "what else?"; and compliment students who come up with examples.

Finally, ask students how they would know they made progress on this scale. How would the class know they are at an 8? How would they know that they are at a 9?

Again, collect specific behaviors students say they should be doing more of, or that they should start doing, and write them down for all to see.

As a class, you will be working on those behaviors.

As you do so, notice and share with the class instances of students already behaving above and beyond "level 7". That normalizes the new behaviors, making improvement the new normal.

Remember also that kids love to be challenged, so don't be afraid from time to time to notice what they are doing right and challenge them to do more of it, with comments such as: "Great work on being respectful, class, maybe at an 8 today. Can you reach a

9?"; "No one has interrupted either me or any of you in the past hour, can we keep it up for another hour?"

Note: in the previous chapter I mentioned that if students choose as criteria vague statements such as "being respectful of each other", it might be a good idea to narrow these criteria down to specific behaviors, such as "not interrupting each other". You can perform the scaling operation outlined in this activity either on the general criteria, if students know what the criteria means in practice; or you can perform the scaling operation on the more specific behavioral indicators, if students are still struggling with the general idea.

Activity Thirteen: Small Progress Diary.

Researchers found that a key motivator of performance is the feeling of making progress in work that is meaningful.

How can we adapt the "progress principle", as it has been labeled, to the classroom?

First, have one lesson dedicated to help students find a school subject that is meaningful to them. Prompt students and encourage them until all have something. You can use age-appropriate and class-adapted variations of the following questions:

- What school subject do you need to know well to become who you want to become?

- What is it that you need to learn to make the contribution you want to make to the world?

- What is it that you are naturally interested in?

Next, invite students to write down a paragraph (2 to 4 sentences) about why the subject they chose matters to them.

Then every other week have a 10-minute period where students can write down any small progress they made in the chosen subject.

Note: see also activity seven in the chapter "Mr. Bear Wants To Be Loved", Progress Milestones.

USEFUL QUESTIONS FOR TEACHERS:

On a scale of 1 to 10, where 10 is fully achieving your goal, and 1 is the opposite of that:

- Where would you say you are at now? (X)
- What is already working which tells you that you are at X and not at 1?
- How would you know you took a small little step further in our scale? How would you know you are one step beyond X?

QUOTE:

A journey of a thousand miles begins with a single step.
-- Lao-Tzu

KEY CONCEPT:

Shrink the Change.

FURTHER READING:

Regarding the idea of shrinking change to make it more manageable: Heath, C. & Heath. D. (2010). *Switch: How to change things when change is hard.* New York: Random House.

Regarding the "progress principle" that is at the core of the Small Progress Diary activity: Amabile, T., & Kramer, S. (2011). *The progress principle: Using small wins to ignite joy, engagement, and creativity at work.* Harvard Business Press.

Regarding the activity Working On What Works (WOWW): Berg, I.K., & Shilts, L. (2004). *Classroom solutions: WOWW approach.* Milwaukee, MI: BFTC Press.

Regarding scaling questions: Jackson, P.Z., McKergow, M. (2002). *The solution focus: The simple way to positive change.* London, UK; Nicholas Brealey International; and: Szabó, P. & Meier, D. (2009). *Coaching plain and simple.* New York: Norton.

Mrs. Raccoon and The Berry Patch

The Way of Change: Finding the Bright Spots.

Mrs. Raccoon is staring at her favorite berry patch, on the other side of the meadow.

She sighs.

She recently saw Mr. Bear there picking berries, and now she is afraid of going back.

Mr. Monkey tells her not to worry.

He declares, "I will make a warrior out of you, Mrs. Raccoon. I will teach you paw-boxing so you can fight Mr. Bear!"

Mr. Monkey starts jumping up and down, very excited.

But Mrs. Raccoon is not convinced.

She is too small to fight Mr. Bear!

Mr. Bear is so big and strong!

In the forest, no one is as big and strong as Mr. Bear -- except for Ms. Elephant.

Ms. Elephant comes along.

"Please, Ms. Elephant," Mrs. Raccoon pleads, "Help me fight Mr. Bear! You are so big and strong!"

Ms. Elephant asks, "Why should I fight the kind Mr. Bear?"

Mrs. Raccoon replies, "Well, because he goes to pick berries in my favorite berry patch, and now I am afraid that if I go there, he will eat me!"

Ms. Elephant chuckles to herself and says, "Mrs. Raccoon, I will not fight Mr. Bear -- but I will walk with you to the berry patch, OK?"

Mrs. Raccoon says, "Great, thank you! No one will attack you, Ms. Elephant. You are so big!"

So Ms. Elephant and Mrs. Raccoon cross the meadow together and get to the berry patch.

Mr. Bear is nowhere to be found.

Mrs. Raccoon observes, "It is not always dangerous to be here. Mr. Bear is not always here!"

Mrs. Raccoon starts picking berries. All the big berries, which she did not like, were gone. But all the small berries, which she did like, were there.

Mrs. Raccoon observes, "I think I can tell when Mr. Bear has just been here -- when the big berries are gone! If he has just been here to pick the big berries, he won't be here again anytime soon!"

"I wonder why he only took the big berries," says Ms. Elephant, smiling.

"Indeed!" says Mrs. Raccoon, wondering about that as she is happily eating berries.

COMMENTS:

No problem happens 100% of the time; what happens the rest of the time? Even a toddler who is having a tantrum must stop to breathe; even chronic pain fluctuates during the day. From a purely biological perspective we cannot be in any given state all of the time.

Exceptions to the problem are episodes when you expect a problem to occur, but either it does not occur or it does in a milder form; by exploring with curiosity these exceptions, you might find seeds of solutions.

For example, a student might be hyper-active; but what is different about the times, however rare, when he is quieter? Is it a specific time of day? Or is it a specific day? Is he quiet when he is with some specific students? Or is he quiet after getting attention?

There is a big shift when you, as a teacher, can go from "this student is always troublesome" to "sometimes this student is troublesome, sometimes she is not too much trouble".

There is room for action.

Activity Fourteen: Noticing The Exceptions.

Psychologists say all of us have a "negativity bias".

That means that we pay more attention to (and we remember much more easily) negative things and events. Any car that cuts you off in traffic is much more attention grabbing and memorable than all the cars that pass you by uneventfully. From an evolutionary perspective it makes sense, because things that go bad are those that require fixing ASAP, whereas things that go well do not require immediate action. However, as one of the co-founders of the Solution-Focused approach, Steve de Shazer, succinctly put it: problem talk creates problems, and solution talk creates solutions. The more we focus on what is wrong with one of our students, the more we find. Conversely, the more we focus on what is right with one of our students, the more we find.

The following activity is designed to compensate for the negativity bias.

Again, it is not about being "positive" but about being balanced; it is about noticing the positive alongside the negative. We do not need help regarding noticing the latter so we focus on the former.

This activity is for teachers only and it does not directly require students' involvement.

Step one: regarding a specific student you are concerned about, start noticing everything he or she is doing right. It might be little things, for example the student sitting down at her desk when the others do, or the student raising his hand instead of interrupting as usual.

Step two: be curious about the times when the student is on the right track. For example, you might notice that an "aggressive" student is such only when an adult warns him of impending punishment, and not in other interactions with adults nor in any interaction with peers. It might be useful to spot patterns, but especially at first, do not be overly concerned about that. Focus instead on step one, simply noticing the good things. That is an important skills to have to apply Solution-Focus inspired techniques like the ones you find in this book.

Activity Fifteen: The Pearls.

This activity is designed to help students build their "noticing the positive" muscles.

The core concept is for students to notice three good things.

Some variations on this theme are offered below; feel free to create your own.

a) Periodically invite students to scan their environment in class and identify three good things. Have some students share them with the class. For example, one student might pick the following: the roof over their head, the candy in their lunchbox and the pencil in their hand.

b) Periodically, as an assignment, invite students to scan their environment at home and identify three good things. They will then report them in class.

c) Periodically invite students to write down three things they would not change about either one of their friends in school or about their own family.

d) Periodically invite students to write down three good things they caught their classmates doing.

USEFUL QUESTIONS FOR TEACHERS:

- Have there been times recently when you were expecting the problem to happen in the classroom and either it did not happen or it was a little bit better?
- What was different about the situation?
- What did you do differently? How did students respond?

QUOTE:

If you are trying to change things, there are going to be bright spots in your field of view, and if you learn to recognize them and understand them, you will solve one of the fundamental mysteries of change: what, exactly, needs to be done differently?

-- Chip and Dan Heath

KEY CONCEPT:

Instead of Analyzing Problems, Find Exceptions to the Problems and Build on Them.

FURTHER READING:

Regarding the negativity bias: Baumeister, R. F., Bratslavsky, E., Finkenauer, C., & Vohs, K. D. (2001). Bad is stronger than good. *Review of General Psychology,* 5(4), 323.

Regarding the activity "The Pearl" and the idea that no problem happens 100% of the time: De Jong, P., & Berg, I. K. (2012). *Interviewing for solutions* (3rd ed.). Belmont, CA: Cengage Learning. "Three good things" is a popular and well-supported positive psychology intervention: Seligman, M. E., Steen, T. A., Park, N., & Peterson, C. (2005). Positive psychology progress: empirical validation of interventions. *American Psychologist, 60*(5), 410.

Mr. Owl Doing More of What Works

The Way Of Change: Do More Of What Works.

It is dusk. Mr. Owl is up early studying his notes.

He observes it all, writes it all down and then studies his notes. That is how he became the wisest animal in the forest.

Mr. Monkey passes by.

Mr. Monkey asks Mr. Owl, "What are you doing, Mr. Owl?"

Mr. Owl says, "I am studying, so that I can become even wiser!"

Mr. Monkey says, "Good. But you should study in the morning. That is what everybody else does."

So Mr. Owl starts studying in the morning.

But the morning is when Mr. Owl usually goes to sleep.

The morning light is too bright for him.

The daytime commotion is too much for him.

His head is constantly spinning: animals going back and forth, birds singing...

After a few days of studying in the morning, Mr. Owl is very tired and very sleepy.

Learning seems so hard now!

Ms. Elephant passes by.

Ms. Elephant asks Mr. Owl, "What are you doing, Mr. Owl?"

Mr. Owl yawns and says, "I am trying to study, so that I can become even wiser!"

Ms. Elephant says, "Good. But you look tired!"

Mr. Owl, "Zzzzzzzzzzz."

Mr. Owl falls asleep!

Ms. Elephant gently puts him to bed. When Mr. Owl wakes up, it is evening.

Mr. Owl had not studied in the morning, so he starts studying right then.

It is easy in the evening!

He is again happy to read and to learn.

Mr. Owl realizes he became wise by studying in the evening.

So if he wants to become wiser, he should be doing more of what works for him -- studying some more in the evening!

Mr. Owl now is even wiser.

You can still catch him studying in the evening.

He lives in a tree, where he also has an office where animals go see him if they need his wise counsel.

On the door, Mr. Owl put a sign that says: "If it works, do more of it."

COMMENTS:

The easiest way to successful change is to do more of what is working.

It might seem obvious, but most of the time people are so focused on what doesn't work that they miss doing more of what works. For example, someone might be focused on the fact that her job is not very satisfying, and therefore she tends to feel miserable. However, there is one bright spot in her week -- Thursday night when she goes out with friends. That alone makes Thursday her happiest day at work. So instead of tackling the more difficult problem of job satisfaction, it might be easier to increase the weekly amount of social activities, such as dinner with friends or dancing classes. Who knows, not only might this person end up caring less about the annoyances on the job and therefore increase her happiness; she might also find a new job! Therefore, build and amplify on what is already working. This reduces the magnitude and the impact of what is not working -- sometimes solving the problem entirely.

Often in my consulting experience I run into the following scenario: a situation where a team leader is totally focused on the one team member that is holding everyone back. That team member is foremost in the leader's mind. Each action the leader takes in the team has this person as the main focus; but what about the others? The truth is that devoting most of the attention to the team members who are working well makes them feel valued; and sometimes it is the best way to get the recalcitrant team member in line.

A similar dynamic might be true in the classroom as well. Some teachers at times might be very focused on the few students that concern them, devoting a lot of effort to them; this is good -- as long as the teacher does not forget the rest of the class.

Last but not least, each person is unique.

Some people are night owls, others are morning larks.

Some people tinker with the new electronic toy without even opening the instructions, whereas others read the whole manual before turning on the new gadget.

What makes you uniquely effective as a teacher?

How can you do more of that?

Activity Sixteen: Doing More of What Works.

The following activity is designed to help students identify successful strategies to do their homework; and to help them replicate those strategies more frequently and more consistently.

Guide the classroom in the following reflection, asking each individual student to write down his or her own answers to the following prompts:

1) Where do you work best on school assignments, without distraction? (or: think of a recent time when you managed to do your homework well. Where were you?). Students might respond with the following replies: "in the library"; or "in my own room".

2) When do you work best on school assignments, without distraction?

(or think of a recent time when you managed to do your homework well. What time of day was it?). Students might respond with the following replies: "mid-afternoon"; or "right after my Mom came home from work".

3) What specifically makes (or made) that time and place favorable for doing homework? For example, it might be any of the following: no TV on; no siblings in the house; quiet environment; had the cellphone switched off; and so on.

4) Once we identify the what / where / when of what worked, now we need to do more of it.

Here is how to automatically craft a plan using the answers to the prompt above:

When it is [answer to question 2],

Then I will go to [answer to question 1],

make sure that [answer to question 3],

and will do my homework.

Obviously make sure that the plan makes sense!

Activity Seventeen: Doing More of What Works, Even If...

You can also go the extra mile and add the following points to the previous activity:

5) Stress to students that even the best laid out plans might find obstacles in implementation. Ask them to answer in writing the following question: What might happen that can prevent you from carrying out your plan? For example, a student might have the following response: "my best friend might call me when I am in my quiet room studying".

6) Then ask students to answer in writing the next prompt: What will you do then to overcome this obstacle? For example, the same student might write down this response or similar: "I can tell my friend that I will call her back later".

7) Students now have a plan to save the plan!

If [answer to question 5]

Then [answer to question 6].

In the example, the plan would be as follows: "If my friend calls me when I am in my quiet room studying, then I will tell her that I will call her back later".

USEFUL QUESTIONS FOR TEACHERS:

- What has been working in teaching to this class? Do more of it!
- How can you do more of what is working?
- If you were to do that, what would your students notice? And their parents? And your colleagues?
- What else would be different?

QUOTE:

One evening an old Cherokee told his grandson about a battle that goes on inside people. He said, "My son, the battle is between two wolves inside us all. One is Evil. It is anger, envy, jealousy, sorrow, regret, greed, arrogance, self-pity, guilt, resentment, inferiority, lies, false pride, superiority, and ego.

The other is Good. It is joy, peace, love, hope, serenity, humility, kindness, benevolence, empathy, generosity, truth, compassion and faith."

The grandson thought about it for a minute and then asked his grandfather, "Which wolf wins?"

The old Cherokee simply replied, "The one you feed."

-- Anonymous

KEY CONCEPT:

Instead of Trying to Fix What Is Not Working, Do More of What Is Working.

FURTHER READING:

Regarding the idea of doing more of what works: De Jong, P., & Berg, I. K. (2012). *Interviewing for solutions* (3rd ed.). Belmont, CA: Cengage Learning. Or any book about Solution-Focus (SF) practice, because this idea is at the core of SF.

Regarding the activity Doing More of What Works: Duckworth, A.L., Gendler, T.S., & Gross, J.J. (2014). Self-control in school-age children. *Educational Psychologist, 49*(3), 199-217. See also my dissertation, freely available here:

http://repository.upenn.edu/mapp_capstone/54/.

Regarding the activity Doing More of What Works Even If: Duckworth, A. L., Kirby, T., Gollwitzer, A., & Oettingen, G. (2013). From fantasy to action: Mental contrasting with implementation intentions (MCII) improves academic performance in children. *Social Psychological and Personality Science, 4*(6), 745-753.

Mr. Buffalo and The Tree Stump

The Way Of Change Three: Doing Something
Different.

Mr. Buffalo is hard at work.

A dead tree fell onto his path and blocks his way!

So he keeps charging at it, to clear his path.

Thump! -- he goes, as he hits it with his powerful
horns.

Thump! -- he goes again.

Thump!

The thumping noise can be heard all over the
forest.

Mr. Monkey sees him hard at work.

Mr. Monkey says, "It might take weeks to break
down this tree, Mr. Buffalo! But it is blocking your
way, so you have to do what you have to do."

With those parting words, Mr. Monkey goes away.

Thump! Thump! Thump!

Mr. Buffalo keeps hitting the dead tree with his
powerful horns.

Ms. Elephant comes along, drawn by the thumping noise.

Thump!

Ms. Elephant could easily take the dead tree out of Mr. Buffalo's way with her trunk. But she knows Mr. Buffalo can make it on his own, if only he tried something different.

Ms. Elephant asks, "Mr. Buffalo, are you making progress?"

A tired Mr. Buffalo replies, "Not really!"

Ms. Elephant gently suggests, "How about trying something different?"

Mr. Buffalo thinks and thinks. He thinks so hard you can almost see steam coming out of his ears.

Then, all of a sudden, Mr. Buffalo starts his charge again, going full speed towards the dead tree.

Ms. Elephant braces herself for the inevitable thump.

But there is no thump -- only a triumphant yay-hee from Mr. Buffalo, who is now on the other side of the dead tree.

He simply jumped over it!

Mr. Buffalo walks away, feeling proud.

They say now he makes it a point to tell everybody: if it does not move, just jump over it!

COMMENTS:

When you are doing something that is not working, try something different.

It seems obvious; yet many times people get stuck doing the same thing over and over again.

When you do something different, you might not find a solution right away, but at the very least you will learn something new about yourself and whatever it is that you are facing.

When you do something different in an interaction, you break a pattern. You surprise the other person and you create the space for other behaviors to emerge. For example, you might be stuck in a confrontational pattern regarding a student's homework. You ask for it, the student says he did not do it; you ask why, and he offers something unbelievable; and you both escalate from there. So try to do something different, anything that your intuition tells you that might be useful. For example, you might praise him for his consistency in not doing things, or for his courage in always challenging you. Or you might acknowledge he did not do his homework, and then move on to other students and only later address the issue. Whatever it is you choose doing, he has to choose how to react, so something new will happen. If useful, do more of that, and if not, try something else.

Activity Eighteen: This, That, and Something Else.

The following is an activity that you can carry out either on yourself or with the class.

1) <u>This, That, and Something Else -- self-reflection for teachers.</u>

Set aside a moment at the end of each week.

Reflect on what is going on regarding your class by answering the following prompts:

a) *What is working?* Write down what you did that seemed to lead to good results, in as much detail as possible. More specifically, answer the following questions: what exactly did you do (or did not do)? When and where did you do that? With whom? In other words, not only capture what you did, but also the whole context in which the action took place. Furthermore, write down how you know that what you did worked. Were students paying more attention afterward? Did they turn in better essays?

For example, you might have noticed that the morning after you went to bed half an hour early, you had more energy, as demonstrated by the fact that you asked lots of questions to students and they seemed more engaged as a result. Or you might have applied a specific teaching technique, say "Cold Call", when teaching English and noticed that students seemed to be paying more attention.

b) *How can I do more of what is working?* Write down a specific plan. When [specific situation outlined in answering the prompts above or similar], then I will [specific behavior that is working].

In the first example provided, the plan might look something like this: "when it is a school night, then I will go to bed a half hour earlier than I do now". In the second example, it might look something like this: "when I have to teach history, then I will use the "Cold Calling" technique too". See also activity sixteen in the previous chapter for additional examples.

c) *What did not work?* Write down specific actions you took that did not lead to the desired results. Include contextual detail, such as when, where and with whom. If you see a pattern of unsuccessful actions emerging, despite attempts at tweaking either your specific behaviors or the context in which they occur, then drop this course of action.

d) *What can you do differently?* There might be issues or situations for which it is really hard to come up with what is working. For example, you might find yourself acting out the same frustrating pattern with a student, as in the example above about the student who is not doing his homework. You might have tried different established tactics, but none seem to be working. At that point, it might be useful to try something different, however weird that something might appear. Who knows, it might work!

2) <u>This, That and Something Else -- in class.</u>

Whenever you think it is appropriate, after an assignment or after a lesson, lead students to reflect on the experience by using the following prompts:

a) What worked? What did you do right?

b) What did not work?

c) What can you do differently next time?

It can be a good idea to do this frequently enough that it becomes a habit for students to ask themselves these questions.

USEFUL QUESTIONS FOR TEACHERS:

- Next time a difficult situation recurs, try something new. What was different? How did others react? What worked?
- What else can you be doing differently?
- What would your friend / parent / sister / brother / role model, etc. be doing differently in this situation?

QUOTE:

The definition of insanity is doing the same thing over and over again expecting different results.

-- Unknown

KEY CONCEPT:

Do Something Different.

FURTHER READING:

O'Hanlon, B. (1999). *Do one thing different: Ten simple ways to change your life.* New York: William Morrow.

What is Solution-Focus? A definition

"We learned a long time ago that when there is a problem, many professionals spend a great deal of time thinking, talking, and analyzing the problems, while the suffering goes on. It occurred to a team of mental health professionals at the Brief Family Therapy Center that so much time and energy, as well as many resources, are spent on talking about problems, rather than thinking about what might help us to get to solutions that would bring on realistic, reasonable relief as quickly as possible.

We discovered that problems do not happen all the time. Even the most chronic problems have periods or times when the difficulties do not occur or are less intense. By studying these times when problems are less severe or even absent, we discovered that people do many positive things that they are not fully aware of. By bringing these small successes into their awareness and repeating the successful things they do when the problem is less severe, people improve their lives and become more confident about themselves.

And, of course, there is nothing like experiencing small successes to help a person become more hopeful about themselves and their life. When they are more hopeful, they become more interested in creating a better life for themselves and their families.

They become more hopeful about their future and want to achieve more.

Because these solutions appear occasionally and are already within the person, repeating these successful behaviors is easier than learning a whole new set of solutions that may have worked for someone else. Thus, the brief part was born. Since it takes less effort, people can readily become more eager to repeat the successful behaviors and make further changes."

-- Insoo Kim Berg
quoted from the home page of the Solution-Focused Brief Therapy Association (SFBTA)
http://www.sfbta.org/about_sfbt.html

About the Author

Dr. Paolo Terni, MAPP, PCC

Dr. Paolo Terni is originally from Italy, where he spent most of his life. He now lives and works in California.

Passionate about helping clients achieve the change they want, Paolo has been coaching executives, leaders, and professionals since 1997.

As a big proponent of brief interventions for achieving lasting change, Paolo has been practicing Solution-Focus (SF) since 2005; and teaching it to other practitioners since 2009, as part of Solutionsurfers International Faculty. He regularly hosts SF training events both in Italy and in the USA.

Paolo holds a graduate degree in Philosophy of Science (Dottore in Filosofia, State University of Milan, 1994) and a graduate degree in Positive Psychology (Master of Applied Positive Psychology, University of Pennsylvania, 2014), both with honors. At the University of Pennsylvania Paolo had the opportunity to work with Angela Lee Duckworth, Ph.D. on the development of interventions to foster academic achievement and character growth in students. He thus became interested in Positive Education and in ways to incorporate Solution-Focus in the classroom.

To hire Paolo to coach you on how to achieve sustainable change in just a few sessions by using the solution-focused principles illustrated in this book, send an email to: *briefcoachingsolutions at gmail.com* or visit his website at: www.briefcoachingsolutions.com.